How To Find All Missing Persons. And Collect All Reward Offers. The Formula. Volume II THE CASE OF TONI TIKI

David Gomadza

www.twofuture.world

PAPERBACK ISBN: 9798325463488

DEDICATION

A better world

CONTENTS

ACKNOWLEDGMENTS

Tomorrow's World Order

 HOW TO FIND ALL MISSING PERSONS. AND COLLECT ALL REWARD OFFERS. THE FORMULA. THE CASE OF TONI TIKI

Send.ya [secretly]
Sendtoyahweh.start
Sendonlyifindangerofdeathorthereisdangerofdeathforanotherhumanbei
ngsothatyahwehknows.start
Now if we are to ask why this is the answer Yahweh records all situations that involve risks of death that why Sergeant Peterson Humphreys keeps sending information to himself instead of Yahweh that means he is commanding you today to kill Toni tiki because today is the say she dies 28 of January 2024 [19 March 1998 in Maraoubrab Sydney Australia British time 22.86.yatime
So you mean a Braun miss is a command in this case yes he is saying go murder the retarded that that calls us retarded in uniform but don't use you dick as planned but use your hands and he complemented on your hands saying if I were you I would squeeze a billion times harder now what this means is that Sergeant Humphreys is giving him the key of his powers the ability to squeeze a billion times harder now what can we say about Sergeant Humphreys in a digital world saying things has become a death sentence you impose on yourself but how can a clever person give a command to kill without anyone else saying anything else this is the challenge so the Australian government devices an ASM system standing for Armed standard Minaimage meaning ability to say things without the need for words or actions but a message that can be understood by all that if someone is to repeat the same then the next person will do exactly the same but without being caught now if we can elaborate on this this means that nowadays the forces are employing

methods to kill that don't involve words commands etc. by brain commands and to make things worse the easiest brain messages ever simply because no human on earth will ever understand this unless he know Yahweh who can tell him what happened now in this case this James pherty once had consensual sex with this Toni Tiki when growing up but realized that she had at the time been raped willing by volunteering to see how many men she can fuck in one session and what kind of wild orgasm she can have why because she had never had an orgasm before and had literally no clue what everyone talked about as Sergeant analyzed her brain scans now if we are to ask what can be of this Toni this is the answer its only a matter of time before she starts experimenting that can lead to her death but again if someone puts herself in danger like this who is to blame if she ends up dead again checking her brain scans she had already been declared as dead at some point by this James pherty but something that was proved not to be true by Sergeant Humphreys who had taken over the case the day of her death she had called this Humphreys asking for help this is the call; Help help you said when I need anything I can call now this is the call if you can hear me someone wants me dead today he keeps sending messages as hidden codes like watch the dark fall on you like thunder and ask who is heaven and hell constantly until something jumped out of me and screamed so loud I literally shit myself otherwise I would not call so here I am I need you so come I swear I cut me into boxes and give you promise get me out of this hellshit I promise I never call you...Toni I go something shouted so loud she covered her ears then everything stopped but now looking at what happened somehow she had made this call earlier on that the times were different but someone clever out there had switch the scans just before death but how is this possible if we may ask Toni had phone several weeks before after James pherty discovered that she had slept with more than 1000 men most of which were homeless beggars James pherty had helped during his course as a police officer when he came to the force he wanted to change things I guess somethings can't be changed so this is what happened to him it was the force to change him not the other way round now if we are to ask what can be of this James pherty then this is the answer its only a matter of time before another person set him up Now this is exactly what happened
Toni left her father's dilapidated house and walked straight to James pherty house there she found out that he had heard about the 1000 plus romp only after he had admitted that he had got her pregnant now as

he tell friends and family as a police officer he discovered that even though it was consensual they had literally fought each other to keep adding the number by repeats to him the repeats represented a form of abuse which if he had his way he would need to use to get everyone of them now that she was his pregnant girlfriend here things become complicated now she started equating him with those men here and there only that he was the only one who did it best because with him she had an orgasm meaning he got the trophy otherwise she can see how different he is from all those because she consented just like with him and they only bruised her which lasted less than a week after that she had forgotten them but him had made it special that to forget was like getting strangled at the same time being given an orgasm okay if it's death that's okay but try to give a woman an orgasm and kill her at the same time he literally choked hearing this he had thought giving her a home and love was to stop the 1000 plus men he said was abuse to her the emotional attachment was killing because he loved her he was not supposed to love her after all that and to be honesty all this was done by the police themselves to protect their own after they realized that he was taken by the case James as a young inexperienced officer only found out about the other men after but the truth is that he knew before that but wanted all the men who did this in jail and Humphreys had pushed him into starting a relationship with her so that when they go after the men they will be brutal enough to literally kill them but now after hearing herself comparing him to the rapist that literally tore his nerves he shit himself there and there and said; God if I knew she would say this I would have killed myself instead and not touch her God kill me for her for I swear you know me I was pressured to punish 1000 men who sleep with a retarded but she said you don't want me because I am a retarded that trigger something I realized it was this maybe that got her into sleeping with all these men now I regret my actions I abuse her just like those to make things worse she said I am the best of all because she squirt with me that hurts like hell I joined the force to clean it but I swear I never had everything blamed on me like this ever one day only me came to work that's how bad this has been now if I may ask what would be of James pherty after this day he would have been thrown out of the force by Humphreys who had already handed him his notice of dismissal after her auntie filed a complaint with the police now what could have been of this Peterson Humphreys? He would have lost his job as the Sergeant only because of pressure but the force had not done anything considered wrong that same day she had threatened to take things further if James pherty was still on the force now let's see what can be of this James pherty on this day he had already been given a noticed of dismissal by Peterson Humphreys but had refused anything from him saying that he had done worse than him and he can prove it but lacked the proof so in such position he was not in a position to tell him to leave the force if that is the case he should leave first now what had this Peterson Humphreys done before he had put this 1000 men in place just buy calling her a retarded that can't cum but one that pukes sperm on sight of men before even being touched she had cried for days because this meant the vagina the only thing she has to bargain with me since everyone calls her a retarded was so weak to puke than to swallow sports that alone meant to strengthen it she needed to be strong to sustain what was ahead of her and this made her arrange a sex for free for everyone which she opted out last minute but had to switch her back without the men involved this made even James pherty stop everything and started blaming Peterson Humphreys for the switch if we may ask what could be of this Peterson Humphreys then this is the answer he could have been the one involved in the switch so that the force have a job now let's look deeper at what happened this Humphreys had made a phone call that was intercepted by James that said that the switch was off and if asked why even talk about the switch when he had nothing to do with the sex that had alarmed James enough to call another police station and report him this only increased the pressure between the force and James now what could have been of James at this day in time he could have been freed from nothing he was free but even if something was on his case calling someone else would have implicated the local police as corrupt outright now if that was true he could have asked Humphreys to be arrested as the one behind the rape so that they go hard on everyone all on false account now let's Ask what could be of Humphreys he could have at be suspended open when accusations leads to suspension that means they are serious and most would need a huge law firm to be reinstated but at s huge cost in financial terms meaning most will resign and get their salary and pension now what can be of toni on this day on this day she could have been saved because a new bunch of officers would come to protect her if loans fail now let's go deeper with this now Ask what was James pherty plan in all this he was going to implicate all those innocent men foe sex foe everyone who had an extra round because she had consented to a short round as okay without any harassment from the organizer who turned up to be the police but everyone to be haunted just for secrecy for a maximum of two years while they round up the culprits now what can be said of James and sex with retards are people over legal limit but act or think like they are below legal limit after being pressured just by being called retarded now let's Ask what could have been of james pherty after all this the truth is that he would have been the most corrupt person in the world because the men had had consensual sex even the extra rounds was at her request she had refused all this Now what could have been of Toni she could have been left to enjoy life and sex and could have easily found a way to cum naturally considering that at the time she was young [ ] Now if we are to ask what was it that the people said they said she would run away no one can look anyone else after such an ordeal but she had stayed now she asked James pherty to marry her which sounded wrong to him that he disassociate himself with her for a strong 8 months by then she had started going after everyone who had slept with her for free expecting to offer her things for free now since he closed on her she realized that he is the only one who had really cared about her but for the same reasons as the others easy sex but it hurts with him because everyone laughs about it and call her crazy genuinely because no one in their right mind will sleep with 1000 men in one night its like a death sentence but surely after that her vagina reading her brain scans became a machine for dicks that will grab literally and announce that you are under arrest because the dick she held would not move when inside her as her rim had solidified after the 1000 plus men a night now if we look deeper a number was put in place 0898365827628598 by Sergeant Peterson Humphreys who wanted her to be happy about fucking men and holding them now what if ask what could be of toni after this she was now to go after every men and have sex with her but now instead of saying you are under arrest now what they did the police would follow her through GPS until she is near house of one of the person them switch off and send police officer but to wait outside hiding waiting for both to come out she would look scared to report them as the organizers but could gain their trust over time to fund the men so that they call her for sake now if we look its like pimps and can be proven because all you need is to prove that they organized [Peterson humphreys' words about her pussy voting from men sperm rather than swallowing it now if we Ask further we can see that they had already started harassing these men on a daily basis providing work for the force that her alone had enabled extra twenty four police officers to be employed to keep eyes on these men but like I

said to keep them quiet but also now to look for work for them to provide money for her so she keeps quiet too now the only person in the way was James pherty who knew what was going on instead of him stopping the men they had actually kept the force on alert to warrant an addition of 24 other officers that meant from hero to the problem that meant that everyone who is knew when he finds out that he got employed by fraud he would resent James pherty for he was the one to prove that they got employed because the girl opened her legs at their gunpoint James pherty had tried to kill himself twice first with poison that he suffered gut problems that ruined his eating habits that in the end he ended up looking like he was sick from cancer but this help all the people involved that they would now refer to all those men who had sex with the girl to go and get checked maybe James pherty had contracted germs from her after they had sex with her Now if we Ask who benefits from all this Now we can see that the hospital would benefit for increased appointments for check up but this would slow down the rate of intercourse between Toni and the men because now they have to be checked first before they have intercourse with her Now if we Ask what became of James pherty he neatly killed himself when one of them men said he gave him an std which he gave to the girl pherty pulled his gun at him snd said who is your doctor I will check first but the men ran away later James discovered that the man was not one of the men but a police officer in disguise that rattled him that he hired a private investigator to put a trail on Humphreys at first only because he was put on the case but later after he was heard saying that the switch was off now what would be of Humphreys after this day Humphreys would have been arrested for such an ordeal on a girl like yoni which they all called as retarded now let's see what could be of toni this day Toni could have been saved because the organizer would have dies in Humphreys now what could be of
after this surely this would have prove that he was to stand for the victims rights by bringing the real culprits himself now let's look at the accusations that James pherty made about the force the force was nothing about a bunch of men and women who used little girls as food for the bait something that he would never do if the force was so corrupt that he is the one who end his life all this come out in his suicide note which he left just before being short in the leg before he jumped over the bridged but if we look closer all this might not be what it is this James pherty went shopping the same day and shopping for clothes to win her back according to his brain scan if it's true that

means the death that followed was not planned unless it was planned to look like that since we are dealing with clever people now if we Ask what would have been of James and toni the answer is nothing this is because toni worked for the police and was recruited to work for them on James after he accused his superiors of corruption which was proved in court earning him as the new broom that was to clean cut all rubbish but this was not taken lightly so a romance between James and toni was highly unlikely but she loved him day of death but Humphreys made sure that this will never happen because that would prove that he was willing to change his life to make things better for women who are orphans but then again the police made her an orphan by putting her in that position when they shot her father a drug dealer named Brian but as was the case those days police are better to parent other people's children's as the general belief at the time now let's look at what can be of the police force having this information they can be pressured to change and adopt a more family approach that the parent not them knows better now let's conclude this mess and tell you our way forward ad Tomorrow's World Order we can look at her death first and come up with our own recommendations now this is how she died according to her brain scans but you might find several versions all which can be proved as real but I read Yahweh's [send

Ya] she woke up early in the morning and checked letters from her father's dilapidated house and said where can I get a huge shag this house is a mess if I had a dick I will fuck all the new police officers I bet all will vomit my sperm but quake like bitches on heat all night when I am gang raped so that they have a job and a loaf of bread and guess what for their kids am I not the bread winner in your own house shuts with hepatitis in the arse who only scratch when it's in not when it itches because when it itches they tense and say they are the bravest we watched our breadwinner make her cum and squirt all over the house on orgasm which they all wished because if I were to squirt then that means it was not a crime but if I had not squitter then all would be in prison a safe place for my mother because all these men would not knock the door for sex and secondly for us girls because not of them but of the police who got our fathers into drugs after giving them criminal records so that they can work and then who literally raped us to orgasm the men they talk about just after a second realized it was a set up but theirs did not and continued until I fell pregnant but can we say it's the men's problem? They take away women of their age who they are supposed to fuck and call them retarded who can be fucked and unleash one to literally kill all if I had not defended the men they would have literally blasted them off and planted drugs I believed my father that is what he had told my mother she only confessed when I refused to press charges against the men men when pushed in the corner do stupid things but none tried to kill me but theirs send secret messages daily with threats if I don't shut it now I will explain in this letter how they talk to us and how they send messages I wish God would listen and prove this because they talk in my brain enough to go outside and see them standing there so how could that be a coincidence God is my witness I just wish one day he would come and say she is telling the truth the real problems are the police not the men after all the men are our fathers for most girls who are to make ends meet or sell their kids to the police for a loaf of bread and get us raped my God I died that day o had refused by the [my eyes blind with something inside me I guess that spin to turn iris inside so that I can't see literally] I was not awake I was dreaming puking seems out like hump says [Peterson humphreys said] he had said this retarded would puke sperm from her mouth but I tell you the men all refused sex they all came in one by one and cried beside me until I puked if I don't puke they don't go out but somehow one of theirs joined the list without permission and was not aware of anything they later said that he was knew and was unaware what they do just to create work so they left but he came back when they all said that she had not come but meaning raped me as a way to say that their job drills was a success and they announced collection of funds from a lot

of business people to provide jobs for the men for ' bail' but after all that had ended one of them realized it was a set up their not for the men but for one of them who was top critic one names James pherty who had joined and refused but kept saying who organised the drill that's so risky enough to physiologically damage a kid just for a loaf of bread but the more he said that the more something happened in my head [it's a original nhs British number 78792869838248 that is designed to imitate physiological damage by continuously worrying about the damaged but there was another men who kept saying you smoking weed man that kept removing it because of this I started resenting him if damage was to happen then it was his fault now having said that looking at all this you can see that nhs [Australian branch called national health services of australia] where the ones behind all this so that they frame in later years using this case where they have just pretended so the companies offer them jobs on sympathy but only that they pay what was not normal pay as minimum wage this means that the police has provided jobs for illegals creating chances for the home office to come and deport everyone and collect real money from the company this was in line with the managers who they will have put in place in the first place most where they don't qualify now you can see a vicious circle of everything illegal enough to power the police force for 20 years now let's Ask some fundamental questions what could be f the police force without all these illegal set up that would catapult everything creating jobs and funding that last only when the hatching price has been reached that of British 8 million when that happens a reward of 1million which is just there to raise awareness but never offered to anyone except where the victim threatened to tell the truth for a cut of the money from a television news agent if the price money is not realised but with severe consequences as the man lost everything to cancer within weeks of receiving the money Now what could be of the judges / people who organised who organised this drill they can stand for murder for every person who died after this drill as cover ups to make sure that they don't talk now let's Ask what can be of nhs then this is the answer l in the end one will open eyes and see it for what it is so that it can be brought to justice for the suffering of women and children but some might argue that they are doing a great job that if one is not a threat he will never be no matter what but can their tactics stand in a court of. of law this is the answer The onus of feeding orphans has meant gapping to drastic lengths but can it be said that it is the one to blame as it uses children as food instead of bait we can elaborate on this by saying that they use people as the bait but not intending to go for the bait itself but for the food nhs has been known to go for people who oppose them meaning the food and not the people they set up to trap now who are the people referred to as the food in this case the only real threat was james pherty who they wanted to get rid if he is the only one who had a motive foe all this but also the person strong enough to challenge this ring of abuse and stop it but getting caught in it enough to prove it but looking at all this it's not just James there was a senior constantly who had raised concerns about the risks involved they had gone one way too far than what was authorized meaning breaching all laws and had cut corners by falsely representing the information to gain a favorable advantage to keep abusing children no matter how they see it its abuse psychologically imagine hearing that a girl was raped by thousand men when it's all lies then find out that it was all a set up and the person they are after is one of their own a whistle-blower who had vowed to protect children but to realize that he was the target now what happened the day she died is shocking now this is the climax you will never hear anywhere else because this is a closely guided secret now this young girl had been a pain to all even the hospital resented her for they had given her mother mouth cancer so that she can talk all this to cover up for their own guilty now the day she died she had agreed for an abdomen test for pregnancy but had changed her mind but the a

Point mentioned had not been cancelled she had tried to cancel it but ran out of credit when she found out that she had run out of credit when someone phoned her she thought it was the hospital and answered quickly before she heard who it was it was the police telling her that she had died during an operation in hospital but she said I didn't go then the line went dead she called a one Peterson Humphreys who asked what was the matter are you pregnant but how can that be mine problem and slammed the phone down saying get fucked for real then call me you waste our time with these silky games to gain attention but when you really need attention no one will ever take you serious now once he had said that he actually sent a message to her using this command

Ask.forhelponlywhenyoursoulexitthebodybecausethisiswhatnormalpeopledo.start instantly a new message came our of her body saying that risk of death run now and hide in hospital ward 10 rescue approaching now just as she had finished talking a huge knock at the door startled her that she literally shit a small piece of human faces that she panicked instead of running g she looked down if anything has fallen down but the door opened and James pherty stood at the door and said your time is up heaven or hell she literally dropped faces in from of her somehow her knickers were lodged to her right left side that some fell on his shoes as he was closer to her he screamed

Dirty where the hell did you just do on my shoes these are alineian shoes 1000 dollars a piece oh you do 1000 for noteall that makes you what she cried hard but stopped crying and said at least I have a dick to fuck all but you if you know none touched me they just pretended to have sex with me so that I have money if I refuse I will say I lied only this one had sex with me I had lied my age as 17 but I was only 13 and none had known and cared because of the switch but during the day there was sex involved but with my mother all would come to me first and offer money to me I would say 60 if he say for a whole like you I would cry so that he don't reduce until he agree then I will spit once I have spit somehow that would remove something they hanged on his dick so that if he goes on to fuck her with me refusing then that thing will be prove that he had sex with her and not her mother now what she is talking about is something I just learned recently as well that God can send anything or humans even souls to any planets but simply attaching the correct binary number so that it's taken to the correct place but this thing of using saliva is not new but had not seen it before in use but might have heard about it but let's look at how things went on that day the rescue was the same as the killer James pherty was to rescue her but they would make her implicate him as well that even though his intention was to make a change now facing what he wanted to do to all those men and realizing that the force went for food instead of bait [the men] he shit himself as well and what happened this day someone called amrtetpsoterstuvwxyz had reported the case to his superior who had said that he must keep an eye on James Humphreys the day she accused him of being the trophy taker he had literally dropped one like hey miss you and death are one this is one that meaning of how he shit himself according to Sergeant Humphreys laughing hard telling Sergeant matroontrenop who had just been transferred there now let's see what happened on this day the hospital pretended to be training her to fight men like James pherty who were in a position of trust but goes on to continue abuse a person like her after knowing that she is called a retarded now let's look at what happened in real time now that we know who was who James pherty knocked on a door on a street with an orange door that looked like red from afar his eyes squinted at first sight he then went in the yard and checked first before seeing a woman on the phone with knickers in her hand now this is what happened he knocked on the door someone else placed the hands on the door handle so that the handle make an angle at the door as the door reached a certain angle the door instantly opened up and she had heard a tip on her shoulder using code 7898386724867132891 that a trigger would visit to pretend to kill her so that she gets insurance money for the trigger when they make him disappear now if we look at what all this is doing is to make her feel special and valuable from a retard she had given jobs to 24 police officers who on earth can create a job like that for people who call her a retarded now this is the catch the helper who was James pherty who was to rescue her was also the target for the insurance scam that he had just foiled James had gone and taken a house when they slept together after arguing that the stigma of calling someone names had caused her low self esteem that she wanted to fuck a 1000 men but according to everyone he could have run away because of disease associated with sex but he did not instead gave her a house but if we look deep we find out that it's Humphreys who kept pushing him Humphreys had gone to the bank separately and requested house mortgages for everyone in the force because if they protect everyone why no one sacrifice one or two requirements for them he had literally said one day you will knock at our doors in distress asking for help instead the next day the branch manager got knives to death by a homeless man if we look carefully this manager had had a quarrel with Humphreys for not complying with bank requirements but related to car parking now say what happened? She shit herself to death using a simply code 78982654321098682834477998800183 this code what it did was to stop her from asking for anything but looking at it now with what I know from God the door handle is the simple trick to this because if you read my book 33 degrees angle designing trajectory death by default [a jfk case] we are dealing with sophisticated culprits who know death in and out I have caught up only because of finding God Yahweh [.Ya] the one all message in risk of death are sent to now let's look at exactly what happened at birth a doctor rstuvwxyz inserted a chip called hm1tropqrstuvwxyz on her lumbar hip in a few minutes without even the mother knowing but she later complained to that hospital the doctor was sacked and she was offered compensation by the courts but before it was issues she was diagnosed of an aggressive form of mental help that she needed care so the hospital wrote to the court claiming that the money was not enough to cover for medical bill instead what the courts should decide is that a cheque must be written to the hospital in the hospitals name instead of her what happens if she misuse the money after all because of her severe mental health she was now in their care and were now the guardians if we look closely we can see that this was a lie once she sued the hospital they all moved swiftly to pit things in place that they money will never come into her hands now what is that was not done she was awarded 250 000 pounds by the courts but the hospital claimed only 20 000 so the question is where is the rest of the money? Now you will be shocked that every men of the 1000 was protesting about the money the courts had given them which now when they press hard to get through lawyers [the man who kept saying to James pherty you smoke weed was a university lawyer hired by a friend of toni after being offered sex if he win but by a blond woman] now if we look at what could be of this relationship it was just something that gives him something to look forward to you but was married and was an fbi agent hired by a simple call using their website that said british shititttt meaning according to brain scans means inside job and no justice to be obtained send your shittiest to stop the most advanced culprits on earth now you realize why she was destined to die the court money now that we know all about the court money now we can rewrite everything in correct order

1 james pherty was hired to kill Toni by the hospital through a text message that read a house burglar stole 250 000 and we can pay you 30 000

Now let's Ask what happened surely a healthy living being will not just die nhs on day of birth to a single parent initiated a longago.start on her life read by book decoding death start.longago.start] Now if we Ask why this is the reason mothers with children die of cancer in less than five years if they can't find another but...now let's Ask why this is so this is because nhs of australia kill single mothers with cancer if they can't find a husband in 5 years death rate 68 per cent above coincidence level now let's Ask what could be of toni after birth she was put on death row after birth simply because she had no father or known father if we look deeper we see that toni agreed to this only to highlight who was her father all the men refused but one but in her mother's case she had more money than him she had just won a court case worth 250000 while the husband a police officer had 10000 but in debt he had tried several times to kill himself refusing for his daughter to go through all this but the hospital had refused now this is what exactly happened with codes

1 code 08983654821098 sent from Sydney Australia to kill in exactly 8 years after birth with option to extend another 5 if need now if we calculate backwards the code was sent on 08102001 from a number called xtrystuvwxyz now what can be of this code if we test on acetate it kills everything by stress but overtime exactly in 13 years time

2 another code was sent to her was 09821000843268109836541089 now what can be of this code it starts damaging all organs by pressure slowly what can be of this code it kills in exactly 5 years if we calculate back this was sent on 08092005 now what does this code do it stops everything moving fast that means they all new and what the ambulance was doing is to follow her and scare her off with sirens all the time to cause maximum stress on the immune system so that she died fast look at the ambulance schedule per day from birth until the day or death

Early Cockrell 7.am

Latemorning 7.10

Wakeup 7.20
Search for life 7.30
Whywait 7.40
Ask.why 7.51
Notme 7.55
Itakebut 7.59
Whyyoudontlistenareyoudumb 8.04
Todieforyou 8.16
Iwasabitchyouknow 8.22
Yousawmeold 8.32
Yousaidbut 8.44
Youwerebut 8.55
Iamyourcleanmother 9.05
Youdontsay 9.50
Iwasbutichanged 9.55
Iwantedtobut 10.07
Iamyoubutyousaid 1022
Whatcanbeofyou 11.00
Whatyhefuckl 11.10
Yousaid 11.29
Askbutwhynot 11.39
Heybeautifulwhathasbeen 11.42
Askhey 11.55
Askwhybut 11.59
12.32
12.39
13.05
13.09.
13.17
13.23
13.33
13.51
13.59
14.07
14.14
14.26
14.33
14.51
14.59
15.21

15.29
15.34
15.39
15.45
15.55
15.59
16.09
16.26
16.37
16.44
16.57
17.06
17.16.
17.23
17.33
17.45
17.55
18.08
18.16
18.27
18.35
18.44
18.55
19.05
19.11
19.22
19.34
19.44
19.57
20.10
20.22
20.33
20.44
20.58
21.02
22.09
22.23
22.34
22.44
22.55

23.59

00.10

Now if we Ask what all this is then I can say that for sure is the most evil form.of stressing a person in order to kill her by the ambulances who ran races of scaring tactics and blasting the horn where exactly she is so that this cause alteration of the brain Now let's look at why the nhs use this tactic it causes 7 critical changes to the body

1 increase stress hormones in the body by 90% and lower quality of life by 7O%

2 Increase stress hormone on top of that

3 it causes brain damage literally so that they are justified in calling her s retard

4 it uses other stress already generated to increase non anabolic enzymes to weaken immune system

5 it uses all energy as they pretend to push her but in fact moving fast so that when she moved fast as well as the ambulance push its her body receiving the alteration all this to push day of death so that it's a quarter less than the predefined so that the time she is at a quarter to the start.longago.start she will have exactly a quarter of her time taken by the police and the ambulance so that they will say he or she was taken by a quarter or used as a quarter if someone ask so that they can cover their backs or not feel sorry for themselves

6 it lowers response rates if asked a question so that they are justified as a retarded

7 it reduces the amount of time she has left with by a quarter exactly Now let's see why they do it according to them and weight the facts they do it to this is their explanation and see which one the courts will adopt and why they do it to protect women and children to warn them when a pedophile is around so that they don't open their legs this is their reasons that means per day there are 120 pedophiles in the area which their never arrested any for that most of which they confess of finding jobs for them if we Ask how they know they say it's a guarded secretly if asked they said everyone is the same and they just know so in the end the court drops this line but recently we have opened the door by proving what they do that they hack first everyone at birth and what follows is what they do to make that like I said they go for the food and never the bait and to make things worse the person who guard ends up dead in their hands so what kind of protection is this we Ask the courts. We can prove that the wrong doing is by one of their own to inflict the trauma because all the other men love enough not to cause

harm or abuse so they have no one to do any harm that's why she can call them names as retarded in uniforms so over the years they have realize that the men will never harm an innocent girl so they always hire their own to do the abuse or the killing or push her on the edge now what can we say about the sirens that can be refuted the shaking they do remotely by using an acetate like xyz that is powered by a handheld iodine sodium water salt dipped in metal iron will cause wriggling that will tear fresh like a paper to leave lesions all over now if we Ask why this is their reasons so that death is not prevented once nominated to die they must be killed by these lethal monsters who will not stop at anything but will actually increase if some threatening to involve externals like the fbi now let's see why they do these things they uses acetate xyz to cause death ulceration that mimic strong long life disease that no one will believe happened over night due to their acetate now if we Ask what can happen to such a person asking the acetate itself the person will suffer irreparable damage because the acetate as it wrinkles it scares all total tissue to remove all feeds that receive and sends food so that permanent damaged is possible this is called fibrioliss and is lethal because anyone with these death acetates will result in death unless they are removed now let's look why they do this from their point of view the managers to stop other who work for them raising concerns about the safety of children they use these time dragging and resources consuming tactics everyday so that staff are literally exhausted so that it's them who complain once they complain they don't complain about the work but will complain about about the orphans saying that they are wasting their time and they are getting abused by their parents while they take drugs and shit themselves this will have created an alibi for them so that if someone tries to report them to the fbi as they start the shittitttt to anyone reporting the government they use the same shittitttt to refer to the parents of the kidd on drugs and shitting themselves now if we ask why they do this this is their reason who wants to be caught doing dirty who better to die look this is how we do it we rape them so that they complain but when they do and win then that is what we do we will have used them to create an opportunity for us to rove that we deserve the money they are going these because this is a waste because they will end up dead if they say the courts say then we say wait and see what the courts say after we finish with them now ifbthe courts have awarded them more than we have asked them the bank will complain about the courts who through away the money and this trigger change in the court system so that by the time the courts know what has happened there will be knew people with no idea of the obvious points and the files relating to the case will have been taken away legal but not returned and excuses will be made and if we looknatbthis case she was awarded 250 000 of having things put inside her baby because her mother was not brave enough to fight for her but knowing from her mother and herself she would have the courage to convince the doctor that she was abused by the doctor abused by doctors cost millions in payouts with great lawyers now after being awarded 250 000 the outs onbeiiòò^{0}0^{00000} medical bills and after that the other payments when they are about to be paid then her mother or herself ends up in hospital and the moneybgets never released now let's do the math ofbthe 250000 she only got 40000 but the rest was either paid and diverted by the police especially Humphreys after he discovered that James pherty who soon bought a house after a down payment if we Ask him what did you do with the money he would say that it was not his if asked the whose he would say the police force now we Ask what is of the police and houses ever heard of a police without a house? They all no matter what will have houses and most paid but there is no trace of how they pay these now this will surprise to find out that what all thisvis about is to pretend to the world that they help homeless people and all retarded but in actual fact they force them out of their own houses into the street and sell the house for a profit but it's good business because the owners since they are retarded they would have get less money the truth and shocking truth is that they use all this money to secretly buy houses all over the area for their police officers or what will be their houses years after they have killed everything and everyone now the truth is that the girl died only because she was next in kin to a house the father owned which was so dilapidated at some point they had ocked anyone from living there for months and the time they were allowed the value dropped 90% the quarter I talked about is used to reduce the value of the land or property until they have reduced value to only a quarter left now this will shock you the deaths as you can see must happen inside the house to declare it a crime scene for years until all related relatives have been killed then at the end the property is sold at auction for always a quarter value now let's look at this case in detail If we are to ask what can be of the property after it has been declared a crimescene then this is it the day she died she had just finished in painting the house and this is what she said

This house will be James pherty when we are all dead can you believe this image he murdered all these thugs to make his wife happy and as well buy cash the house now this could be speculating but let's go back and check what became of the house you will be shocked to find out that the house was later bought by the rescuing officer

James pherty who owned it until 2021 when it was sold for 278900 to the police office housing association and guess what they do for a living search for dormant houses once crime scenes and buy them back what a business and guess what is the 1000000 reward going to be used for if worn to buy a house that was once a crime scene this time only that they were not involved but wait a minute let's look at the facts again the owner was killed by the hardest to kill or cure covid strain if we look at the details the strain was an unidentified form that only kills woman and her child the owners and leave all the lodges untouched even the new occupants who are all police are so immune they can't be touched by it but this thing is so lethal to reduce the value of the house by exactly a quarter now lets talk about toni tiki' death and what happened after that the day now let's look atvthe cause of death according to the death certificate but its missing and they are still offering a reward for the solving of the case and it's a whooping 1000000 but like I said this money is to make someone buy a house they will lose that means that someone is not one of them? Now let's look deeper at this case with an open eye they advertised that they will pay someone 1000000 for solving this case that means they are asking who wants to die for a 1000000 bet because they bet they reduce your life by to a quarter before the price money is due to collect but in most you will gave died by then now the proof is this when toni was born she had on average

100 years minus being born to a single parent reducing her life by a further 8 years now if she is to leave in she will die when she is approximately 92 years on average but being with a mother with cancer that further reduces her with a more 7 years now we have 85 years now if we need to be fair all they need is a quarter left that means from daybof birth they had already worked out that they need her dead at age 15 or better at 14 years ago now how can you can someone without killing her physically unless if you are traine to kill using digital codes now you will see whybthey offered the mother 250 000 to keep her quiet if she was to expose them it will be life in jail without pararole because they are secretly inserting a death causing weapon to kill this girl meaning caught in the act of murdering the girl now let's look at the real facts what the mother could and could not have proved

1 she could not prove anything that she is hacked and they want to kill her

2 she could not prove how they were going to kill her and her daughter

3 she could not prove that ita the system behind the hit and ran that had killed her father

4 she could not prove that it was them killing women and children for houses to lower their value by a quarter for their service men and women

5 she could not prove that their acts were malicious in nature
She could not prove that it's them who were called shittitttt but her [mother]

6 she could not prove that they are all evil and it's not help but making sure that they clean them

7 she could not prove thatbits them draining their energy with 80 sirens per days above all minimum noise decibels in any country

8 she could not prove that it was them running Rampage claiming titles of who dispose of a kid fast

9 they were not known then for treating women and children for food as everyone believed they went for the bet anyone who go for food and not beat has other motives other than food in most case

10 they would not have stopped then because evidence was for

them unlike now with Tomorrow's World Order documenting all cases in black and white for all to see

Now let's look at some critical questions from all this will the judge then believe our account if we had presented all this as a case against them now they would have thrown it out for having no basis on several grounds

1 the police and ambulance are in a position of trust and must be respected as such

2 the would have argued that it's not possible for those in a position of power to abuse minor or children for food as its against what they stand for

3 will have raised suspicious argument and doing the same on us

4 will have started asking about us

5 will ask what if

6 will ask what can be of us

7 will ask what will be of us

8 will do a search on us as well

9 will prove they are innocent even if they are not simply because there is no way to prove

Now let's Ask what would be of them to be honest now they are in a position of weakness the houses they have accumulated even if open to them have become just like any crooks and to make things worse all the women defend the men for the right reasons the men is a way of surviving the jungle for them its a choice now worse as we have found out that it's not for bait because the bait is clean but to secure finding for houses as such a these houses once own by victims who died in their hands must be confisticated by the courts with immediate effect and returned to distance relatives now if we Ask what can be then you will see that the regime has lost control by doing it in front of the camera where all eyes are there to see Now what could be ofthe police with their targeting of people who complain about them time will come when some within the force will not look for food but for justice against this clever robbery of houses of victims to fund and help their own now if we are to ask what can be of the police houses if all with victims who were in their hands are not returned we will cry justice for the victims until heard now if we Ask what can be of the force with their targeting of women and children foe food then it's also a matter of time but as you can see with their tactics of using illegal tactics like viruses and crushing... then there can never be peace now that I mentioned this

We might as well go deeper and look at the killing and how we can apportion blame if any now the time was set already using a simply start.longago.start what was left was a code that can make things real this is the code 89287648210982748611098728910 once that code was received it silently removed every predefined template in her digital system sustained by a diode code 8238489678284410971652 which is a Siemens hard type rotary propeller implanted on 28 of May 1991 at st Andrew's hospital ward 9 Queensland Australia or obtained there as the source of supplies to other hospitals signed by a one Ajrmatrol now this is prove why the doctor would award the family 250 000 when they complained but then it would have been difficult to prove its real use this propellers use is to end life in a faked suicide attempt by concealing everything this is how a rotary propellers on a human body create the centrifuge effect that means things can flow in any direction meaning even opposition to the norm that means that a body can easily start dropping shit literally instead of someone pushing it now this is all what happened controlled by this propeller alone the way its operated is by remote electromagnetic waves which are HTZ type8 which needs a current of 5amps it uses x-rays gamma and violet for transmission rotating as alternating current so that it can't be detected We created an Electromagnetic Wave Inductive Current to detect this rotary propeller check here click this link
Playback the video and say hello for more details
https://youtu.be/RXaALKUK7B8?si=pCJtwN0XKxmPcQNa

 now if we Ask what can be of the police without the girls they use as bait if you look at the impact this fake had the you understand that means it has generated 8 million dollars and the offer of a reward is proof to that but there are other things to consider as well which we can't ignore given the heavy circumstances of the case now let's look at how toni died she woke up and looked herself in the mirror and let the loudest scream anyone can make she fell on the floor on her left side she instantly woke up and tried to get up but failed that was all needed for code 0892548683829821856721984861178 to work she fell asleep but instantly a huge knock at the door made her to open her eyes but she could not open the eyes code 06987658219838264581928180 was active now all she could see was a shadow like thing blinking she said who is there are you James pherty because your number is blinking instantly something clicked as if there was some voice recording device that started and stopped but only when it's his voice talking he stopped and looked around but what was happening was that the code 0892548683829821856721984861178 was active this is the one that made the clicks that confused James pherty to make him think that it was a recording of some kind now if we ask what had happened she was digitally sedated by code 8298685498786654210 now what can we say about where the code came from James pherty 's style of opening the door had made her brain to freeze and there are several commands that were predefined and determined and here they are and their uses

1 7868983821685543210 to incapacitate her legs so that she can't run

2 code 8498683218456890 was used to make her say silently in her brain if risk of death choose heaven or earth

3 code 897768321983216817 was used to make it look like she made a call to a one Peterson Humphreys saying that "hi I was just to ask you to look at my number and say what can be done but it's all good because you coppers think I am a pain but I think when someone is set up with you then when I am in need of help you must comply now if we Ask what was of toni at this time its not her but just messages being triggered by the codes a closer look at where the codes came from reveal an already stashed put in box with all codes about her that can be used to call back any codes in actual facts it uses a call back code feature using these commands

1 ask.why

2 Ask.whatif

3 ask.whatwas

4 ask.whatcanbedone

5 whatistobedone.start now after this the codes were digital codes in order

82369874568432893867210981O

88336699778877685 [ask.whatcanbe]

77986838264890 [what could be]

77889838764869821

7766859838207788992861789928480

778928521683827588992813254 8

983289764862897896838 20

 Now what can be of humans and digital numbers

Humans can ideally send codes 869838600983820

819838628678983

898929807654386

8877665544433889

88776644332211O1891028645

7788665544281098

2809838677286210

1864982863217498210

7738619210286771021

3678198262498387283

11867928349058678912

28763829871185283292

18776655443322110018928654

77286283219838678910

779838628518466772863869828 7

19876486992871845528 9

77867728648698327810

28928617854983212981807 2

662898386487983210028 6

2895678901236628798

77862832219872863842 1

7728638798210 48399180

77889928577103852102 89

18611778677386189234180
26348678928764589018328
268771892834967718428109

Now we can say that what happened to toni was not expected by anyone even James pherty who was originally sent to kill her knew nothing of the kind of death she would experience now on the floor each of the above codes one by one would activate and in turn switch off everything at a time now according to the brain scans this is how she died as caused by the above codes
1 brain dead at 22.38
2 Liver swell at 22.39
3 abdomen death 22.40
4 gall bladder death at 22.41
5 anus death at 22.42
6 mouth death at 22.43
7 p death at 22.44
8 aspirasophaghs death at 22.45
9 genitals death at 22.46
10 hearing death at 22.47
11 feelings death at 22.48
12 heart death at 22.49
13 vagina death at 22.50
14 one first and last orgasm at 22.51
15 one last breath at 22.52
16 one last breast massage and death at 22.53
17 one tonge kiss at 22.54
18 one last vaginal massage at 22.55
19 one last closed mouth kiss at 22.56
Now that she is technically dead one last vaginal penetration to say goodbye to the most fucking fuck I have met and the best sending off to hell the best neck squeeze of all time and full vaginal penetration and billion times vaginal grip that Humphreys could not take out his dick at first and joked about it saying that what a fucking sending off but she once to go plugged in heaven as if to tear my dick but hey who ever is behind this is a psychopathological cunt meaning closing can't hole even before I

started the hole is closed already British be British but they have taken one step to robbing tombs literally this can't be expected of a civilized people to rob not just their fucking house for the police at dick point but stealing life of a retard like this as if she is the queen is like bending down all men and say queen where are they I can't find not even a single Australian men willing to fight fir their women or even their property her Majesty is stealing not just land in Australia but young lives my God today I enjoyed sex as vagina is supposed to be tight and every inch gripping but I died also today I am glad I never had a daughter other wise I am prince Phillip fucking not the queen but the Queen's daughter

Now we can analyze what really happened this day she died a lot of things happened in Australia during her Majesty visit prince Phillip had just died a year before but had not been sent to heaven as the heaven option was removed now how do they send the prince to heaven this is the ritual to send him to death. Now we Ask why this case has anything related to prince Phillip he grew up in that city name but in Germany maraoubrab Germany and had sacrificed a girl to get money for a house just as they had done if we are to ask then what is to do with the sex then this is the answer he was a Duke but needed accommodation without any money and they had to kill a family and take their house and this is exactly what had happened here the final sending now somewhere else in England the same ritual is performed at the same time and everything is synchronized so that whatever happens there happens there as well and the place is Somerset where constable argetes changes hands for a body with a marine who had died but just for the sending and penetrate a corpse so that when it happens they both be in heaven at ghe same time now if we look at the case of the missing Toni Tiki and that of Asrtes Amgenst in somerset England the cases are literally identical it can be a coincidence especially when everything happen at the same time.

That means it was never James pherty from the word go it was their senior police chief Peterson humphreys [Constantine Artertes Artes] who made it look like it was his constable or sergeant James pherty [

Antonio Burgess] Now what can be said about this case it is the longest case and hard to solve because nhs covered all its tracks and why it's herald as a master piece is the fact that no one can ever satisfactory solve it but us now let's look at the facts between the two cases

1 both by the police themselves for food

2 both for food and not bait

3 all had houses to be taken

4 all had young daughters at the time

5 both had drills involving a 1000 men

6 both had an officer who play hero but end up being involved and accused

7 both had vicious predators who wanted it all

8 both had aspects of violence against women

9 they are all to help the police secure funding through sympathy and never due to ability

10 they both have the same aurora effect where the change in tempo Detect the pace of the story

Now if we are to ask what can be of the two cases then this is the answer they both have the same setting and act all to be the future of things

To be continued

THE FUTURE: INTERVIEW IN AFTERLIFE

On this night I went out and left the party early because of period pain
sometime in January then I walked and saw a car following then the car
approached me the driver acting as if I was a hooked and flashed lights
he then said; hi
I looked down to see his face and he said jimmiboy your only fucking
husband okay I don't have to repeat this again now if you excuse me I
have some bad guys to catch then he drove back to the hostel I knew
he had had that I was seeing a new man in Timothy Frances but he was
scared of James pherty then I said leave him alone he refused me
tonight because of you but I still want you he said okay if you still love
me then I take care of him he reverse to go back but I held to the open
window panel but he had not noticed that he swange very hard and I
literally flew in the air and hit my head hard I think everything broke as
I just passed away and woke up where someone called davidgomadza
woke me up
St who?
Who are you checking on us I am the guardian of the galaxy I am
entrusted to protect the family as per the will of toni tiki
I left 12am I walked for 20 minutes then I saw the car following me
and it was James pherty he was now the constantable of maraoubrab
what happened to Humphreys do you know Humphreys [hump with
clitoris stimulation] he got sacked what happened to your father's
house Humphreys was my father I had no idea what happened to the
house i think James pherty bought it but kept it for some time
The night of death I went out on my own but mate a guy called malvin

Jacob's or something he said I will walk you home then went back for his jacket.....I think he is the one to find me but I was dead but I remember someone saying Wakeup go to afterlife

Can you say that James pherty killed you for a reason?

I loved him but cops bad decisions all the time. I think it was my fault I upset him for reminding him about the fake drill about 1000 men and this time he took it to the heart I was going to leave him anywhere he had become obsessed with the insurance money what insurance money I had taken a life insurance policy for my kids atalps insurance australia it was worthy 700000 dollars can you say that he killed you for the insurance money? He loved me how can you say that it was my fault an accident he could not have it was not...is Shannon okay? I think so

What were you wearing on the night of death a top jump suit orange badge top black ladies trousers and red knickers because of periods make her new again

What do you like to do

I want to have sex with James

What colour of eyes bluhair colour ginger but towards blonde

Any tattoos I swear by ... on neck all round from right to left

Who he swear by according to tattoo.. laughs..[me] any special meaning hide meaning ..laughs...that vagina can grip all dick and ask whatthefuck...laughs I was good so I am told but I only heard sex with James pherty everything else I swear were drills the 1000 men was a drill that's why I fall with Shannon when she found out at point I thought of killing myself I think I feel more happy in afterlife than where I was sleeping now just for the record tell me you full name date of birth and date of death and the names of you kids and their father if you will that will close the conversation yes I am toni tiki I was born tornado tikmore but I couldn't understand why my father would name a beautiful daughter like me tornado so I secretly hated him for that that I will whisper in my dreams having grown up without a father I then started looking for him when my mother got terminal cancer that's when I found out that he was the retarded pass of shit who made my mother a prostitute so that he had a job a nearly blasted him with a gun but I swear James pherty stopped me he tried to control me but after organizing a 1000 men to rape his daughter I never looked at him again ever I stopped talking to my own daughter to preserve her I just hope...tell her I love her I swear I was going to make it up to her then Jimmy just shouted hell and something ran out of my body so fast that night that I literally jumped in the air and fell hard hitting with my head

because what left running out was so heavily my head followed it and I landed back with my head and he drove over me once I s... myself he opened the car door and he said 2 chances only at birth to buy time and at 13 years when you are useful to the force for every female even the princess ask her say whatthefuck.princess as I die I heard something talk inside me it said the fuck is that we are all bitches at one point I just looked up and saw God himself and said Jesus better kill all men I am a princess why I take when he can take if you take where you put them in the end save no men let them die to save them be like God he let men kill his son but to save them I choked my last breath and I heard a voice say behold heaven but you killed a lot of men because of selfishness therefore I reject you .Ya but another voice said go to afterlife instead give her silkpasty 500 for strength and to erase the memories and instantly I worked up on earth I saw everything and heard a voice say 2 seconds left but when I looked at my hands they were black I cried and said I am so dirty I turned black some loved and said you use my body to restore and test everything before you go to afterlife
God on earth is black I saw my self in afterlife

CONCLUSION

The first life of Toni Tiki that took most of this book was just a police drill to get at least 8million in funding of which 1 million they will use for the reward. That means she didn't die at 13 years old but went in hiding. James pherty had told every before that she had died that was a lie now at 26 thirteen years more we find her with James on a night out. I assume she was to convince the man to go home with her knowing that James might follow and let James kill the man but I guess her being her she decided to save the man that he returned to pick up his jacket James furious that she decided to save the man shouted hell startling and frightening her spirit. But is the spirit so powerful.
Hell. Go pick her up and throw her in the air.
I can't you will kill her she is your wife
Soon my deceased ex wife for 780gs go
But James I am your brother you are not But why I keep hearing the message that James is your brother.
Okay if you do this you are my brother but first check who keeps telling you that James is your brother who is listening
James whisper asking nothing James you start again with this force of

gravity He stopped and looked at her You don't believe me he will send you to hell then you will believe in me

Instantly a gusty wind lifted up and entered her instantly lifting her up in the air before she fell down she hit the head hard breaking literally on the spot

James stood there silently

It's finally done I am a constable now Humphreys if it's you you are sacked for getting your own daughter killed who is as stupid as you? She challenged me [force of gravity] he said I have gravity at last there is nothing we can't do even you.

She said you can't do me with your force of gravity so that night to prove a point she removed me by saying if you don't mind we have some sex to do bye go back you are dismissed she bent and knelt to speak to me as if I was a kid that offended me but I was up and I left but next day she is all smiles that he could not get it up and if I Ask why and how come this is the answer she coughed and thrown up saliva but quickly said it's a mistake he said with force of gravity that means again he is the one needed help always this raged the man that for the first time in the history of mankind I turned into him and he felt it all night he kept saying come but she refused after noticing the rage of an animal. After this day she never bother ask him so if she need sex now she started going to the club the Mayfair then on that night she had it coming that I said I swear I will send you to hell and I meant it but it was a joke for him that he tried to send me instead I never spoke to him after that but he ran away from her that night could he had saved her why even asked that you don't know the use of the force of gravity tell me force of gravity can send a real person to Yahweh by a simple coded send.shititttt.hell.ya.davidgomadza.ya

What do you want here? Davidgomadza sent me yes .Ya We need vocabulary eletatetetey

Yes agree [Yahweh]

ABOUT DAVID GOMADZA

Visit www.twofuture.world

How To Find All Missing Persons. And Collect All Rewards Offers. The Formula. THE CASE OF TONI TIKI